Chapter One

Is it possible to describe the details of the invisible person? Well, no. What follows is a journey of discovering the details of the invisible person. You may ask, "Why is it a journey"? It may surprise you to find details about yourself, which you may have or may never have considered and yet you may find yourself, as I did, discovering the person you are, the invisible person.

Is it possible to literally prove the invisible person actually exists? After all, what proof could possibly be presented to demonstrate the invisible exists at all? As this is an excellent point, perhaps the starting point is to examine the possibility that there is nothing but a physical world, which generally arrived into existence by chaos. Yes, let's do that.

YOU MAY BELIEVE THIS ENTIRE BOOK HAS TAKEN A PHILOSOPHICAL WRONG TURN. If you will forgive the apparent wrong turn and continue on this journey of discovery, I believe you will find no wrong turn has been made. I suspect you will find yourself exploring this "nothing but a physical world" approach to life quite differently.

Life itself is certainly a journey worthwhile.

Chapter Two

Let's explore "There is Nothing but a Physical World."

First, this has nothing to do with religion or philosophy. This part of the journey is entirely about exploring the statement: There is nothing but a physical world. If a person is to believe this statement to be true, are there any other statements, which must be held true?

Since only the physical exists it seems there can exist nothing non-physical, which is commonly called invisible. Yes, I believe this must also be held as true in accordance with the first statement. Then, if anything exists which is actually invisible, the first statement can no longer be true. The "first statement" refers to: "There is Nothing but a Physical World."

Note: Visible must include all forces which are only knowable for people who believe "There is Nothing but a Physical World" as something visible was actually affected. Forces of gravity, momentum, magnetism must be allowed as accounted-for in the explanation of "There is Nothing but a Physical World". You must grant this for now as even air is considered to have substance yet seems apparently non-visible.

The Invisible Person

Chapter Three

All forms of intelligence must therefore be merely visible chemical or physical actions and reactions causing human intelligence, human thought, human ethics, human beliefs, human perception. In fact, any action or reaction by a human, an animal or even a rock may be completely understandable and explainable: know-able.

To know completely is not the same as to describe a subject to be know-able. To claim there is nothing but a physical world and describe all subjects to be completely know-able is to describe a hope to some day know a specific subject completely. Know-able is not a statement of already having complete knowledge (of a subject). It is only a claim that possession of complete knowledge is possible (for that subject).

Intelligence and knowledge cannot be invisible (hence, must be visible).

Perception of sound or sight cannot be invisible.

Beliefs and ethics cannot be invisible.

Free-Will cannot be invisible.

Desire cannot be invisible.

Family cannot be invisible.

Community cannot be invisible.

The Invisible Person

There can be nothing invisible about personal feelings or sharing a personal experience.

Life cannot be invisible. Death cannot be invisible.

Language and communication cannot be invisible.

Math, logic or reason cannot be invisible.

The concept of a perfect circle cannot be invisible.

The concept of self cannot be invisible.

The imagination cannot be invisible. A dream cannot be invisible.

A law cannot be invisible.

A religion cannot be invisible.

A philosophy cannot be invisible.

Healing cannot be invisible.

Nature & natural causes cannot be invisible.

A disease cannot be invisible.

Numeric symbols cannot represent anything invisible.

Verbal sounds cannot represent anything invisible.

Written symbols cannot represent anything invisible.

Human perception of taste cannot be invisible.

The Invisible Person

Human perception of smell cannot be invisible.

Human perception of touch cannot be invisible.

Matter itself cannot be invisible. Perhaps energy and space itself cannot be invisible.

A goal, a resolve, a plan, a campaign, a war, a battle, a pledge, honor, self-worth, dignity, hate, love, pity and so many other words cannot be invisible.

How many of the above statements do you hold to be true? One? None? All of them? It is surely your decision and yours alone to decide whether you will accept "There is Nothing but a Physical World" or reject it. If you decide to accept, make sure your decision is visible.

Chapter Four

If you care to explore the best author of "There is Nothing but a Physical World," I find no author to exceed a "Great Books" author named Lucretius. Enter his assertion willingly and try your best to find your way out. Make your best effort to find a hole, an exit.

Perhaps you do attempt an escape from the grip of Lucretius. I attest there is no way out. I do believe there is a way to defeat Lucretius, to declare with complete confidence to be correct, that Lucretius is quite incorrect. But the only way to accomplish this is to acknowledge there is at least one invisible aspect of the human person.

If there is no knowable self-evident truth, then, can the first statement be self-evident? Is the concept or truth, the discovery, the idea that "There is Nothing but a Physical World" be so hardened into the physical body of the human person to be undeniable? Or is human perception of the physical world the beginning, the origin, which must first be acknowledged to exist?

The question has now been put forth. Is there any self-evident truth? Is there any subject considered known with no other basis to know it as true, other than to describe it to be self-evident? If so, is it visible or invisible? If invisible, then there is more than a physical-only world.

Either we continue to struggle to maintain human perception of sound is entirely physical (and therefore

visible), or we allow ourselves to know as self-evident that human perception of sound is invisible.

Suppose we stubbornly remain committed to deny the existence of a physical world.

Chapter Five

Here we attempt to stubbornly maintain there is nothing but a physical world.

Popularity, for the idea or against the idea, is not considered valid, so a vote shall not be held.

To demand an affirmative statement replace "There is Nothing but a Physical World" would merely result in changing the statement to "There is Only a Physical World."

Consider this: If you line up an infinite number of monkeys in front of an infinite number of typewriters, one monkey will type out the entire Declaration of Independence word for word with proper punctuation and spelling. You can't disprove it, therefore it must be true.

What should be obvious is this: Just because I cannot prove it or disprove it does not make it true. Similarly, the description of the monkeys above cannot be disproven, but neither can it be proven.

There is no way to prove or disprove the statement: "There is Nothing but a Physical World."

In present times, the theory that matter is energy means there is no physical world.

Chapter Six

There must be a way to remain stubborn and maintain there is nothing but a physical world.

Consider there is nothing but a physical world. Consider this awe inspiring truth to be more significant than anything in existence. Let's immerse. Let's submerge ourselves.

First things first. The truth must be recorded.

Next, the truth must be shared. Everyone must be convinced that this is in fact the truth, the real way to see the world. This is so important that it must be taught to the offspring of mankind.

But all of this must be done in strict accordance with "There is Nothing but a Physical World." It is OK to record the truth using any material to record the truth. An ink pen and paper is good. To stay in strict accord though, the ink dots cannot represent anything invisible. As long as all ideas, thoughts, character symbols for letters and punctuation marks are only derived from physical events, it is OK. Nothing invisible may be used. All ideas must be physically formed and have physical results. All written letters and words used to record the truth must be physical results and represent no invisible concepts or meanings. Anyone reading the record must ensure all reading only occurs through physical results.

There is risk the record might be considered a form of invisible communication between the writer and the

reader. All care to avoid this must be considered. If communication were to suddenly become invisible somehow, it would be the end.

Next, to share the truth. However sharing can be done, it must be done physically. Because sound might be confused as invisible, great caution to share the truth verbally is advised. If verbal communication is to be used, the sender of communication must be sure all sending activity is completely physical. All verbal and non-verbal communication must remain in compliance with the truth. The receiver must also receive all communication physically. No verbal or non-verbal communication tools can have any invisible aspect.

And hence, the world shall be better than before.

Chapter Seven

Why does it matter? If it does matter that the truth, "There is Nothing but a Physical World," be shared around the Earth, is the idea clearly a physical event?

If it does matter, why does it matter?

It seems the truth, "There is Nothing but a Physical World," should provide an answer. Who seeks this answer? Why? Does the concept of a person actually exist in the physical only world? If there is only a physical world, are there any thoughts? Is there free-will? Is there life? Is there a self? Is there an imagination? Is there desire? Is there perception? Is there pain? Is there suffering? Is there beauty? Is there family? Is there pleasure? Is there war? Is there fighting? Is there a country? Is there a law? Is there knowledge? Is there understanding? Is there wisdom? Is there logic? Is there disease? Is there love? Is there hate? Is there purpose? Is there meaning?

The question more significant than any of the questions above is: Is there a person?

A person must be an invisible person. If the invisible person does exist in some small way, it is enough.

If there is no invisible person, there is no reason to record the truth that "There is Nothing but a Physical World." There is no obligation to share it, to not share it, to think it, to believe it, to love it, to hate it. If there is no person, nothing matters. Even a simple obligation to

share the truth must allow the obligation to be invisible or remain completely meaningless.

Is the concept of person really that important? Existence itself depends upon the existence of the person? Without the invisible person there is no existence? Yes! Correct!

Is it possible there is nothing but a physical world if the invisible person does exist?

If I slap someone and then explain it was a sequence of pinging particles that merely resulted in the slap, and expect to escape all responsibility, that expectation is unrealistic. Although this sounds like a great way to escape all responsibility for the slap, it also removes all the pleasure. Where is the fun in that?

Responsibility only exists if there is free-will. Free-will is an attribute of an invisible person.

Chapter Eight

Is there any hint of the invisible to actually exist and therefore destroy the statement: "There is Nothing but a Physical World."?

If there is nothing invisible, there is no need to respect a living thing. Not even self.

If there is nothing invisible, there is no law. No natural law. No human law.

If there is nothing invisible, there is no knowledge.

If there is nothing invisible, there is no education.

If there is nothing invisible, there is no family.

If there is nothing invisible, there is nothing personal.

If there is nothing invisible, there is no meaning.

If there is nothing invisible, there is no life.

I could say to you:
You are an ugly, ignorant, apathetic, insensitive, unfeeling, unimaginative, unwise, worthless, pathetic, useless, lifeless bag of air. Whether I am correct or incorrect is not the question. The only question is this: Is there any use for the first word? Is there actually a "you"? If not, then it is impossible to issue an insult.

If there is nothing invisible, there is no person.

Perhaps you may feel this chapter is a waste as it appears to be merely a repeat of the prior chapters. However, I believe the prior chapters have provided sufficient evidence for any person reading this to easily conclude there actually is more than merely a physical world. What we just explored is a process. A process of comparing what each of us already knows to be self-evidently true against a proposed view of the world which contradicts what we know to be self-evidently discovered truth.

Chapter Nine

Is it enough to discover or rediscover there is in fact an invisible person? Is it enough to destroy the assertion, the assumption, the theory "There is Nothing but a Physical World"?

I believe an example from William Shakespeare's play "The Merchant of Venice" may provide an answer with sufficient flare. As the character Shylock tells the court that he did desire to collect his "pound of flesh," just before Shylock's approved debt collection, the court exclaimed, "Wait!" If there is nothing but a physical world and a debt is a debt, then a debt collection is just a debt collection. It is just business. But the court suddenly saw through the debt collection scheme. The court revealed an awful insight that Shylock desired his "pound of flesh" to be from around the heart of the Merchant of Venice.
The court then clarified the contract, the debt collection bond, to declare Shylock may collect his bond of a "pound of flesh" but not a measure more and further, not a drop of blood.

Perhaps the message was the nature of a contract wording and Shylock should draft his wording more carefully. Perhaps the message was about revealing hidden intent and then creating hurdles to thwart the hidden intent. Both messages are possible and likely considered the most important message(s) by some.

For me and in context to this chapter, the message is that Shylock attempted to destroy a person (his competition by the way). If there is nothing but a physical world, then how could it matter whether a person is destroyed? If there is an invisible person, who does matter, who does have value, then to destroy the invisible person surely does matter.

If it does matter, if it is considered wrong to destroy a person, is it also wrong to damage a person? Right and wrong come from responsibility, which comes from free-will which is an aspect of the invisible person.

The message from Shakespeare's play does reveal a wrong-doing by Shylock upon the Merchant of Venice. There is another wrong-doer which we cannot allow to escape. Within the paragraph above is a short sentence, which reveals a hidden character "behind" Shylock which also attempted to kill the Merchant of Venice. The sentence, "It is just business" describes a character just as sinister as Shylock and just as deadly.

Is it enough to declare Shylock a wrong-doer alone? Or is it proper to address his accomplice as well? It may seem petty for me to "over-value" the "It is just business" idea as an accomplice as though it has life with free-will and therefore responsibility for its actions. It seems a stretch to describe "person" attributes to a thing.

In fact, I am describing that exactly.

Chapter X

If the character, Shylock, from the William Shakespeare play "The Merchant of Venice" had an accomplice, shouldn't the accomplice also be found at fault for the crime? What is the name of the accomplice? I will name it "legal debt collection instrument."

It seems at first odd to assign the "legal debt collection instrument" an accomplice. Perhaps odd, but I maintain it is appropriate. If it did attempt to destroy a person, then it is an accomplice.

What about "There is Nothing but a Physical World"? Did it attempt to destroy a person? In fact it attempted to destroy all invisible persons. All that remained was unanimous acceptance around the Earth.

If law made "There is Nothing but a Physical World" an enforced or imposed belief, then destroying the invisible person has the full force of government.

How is it possible that "There is Nothing but a Physical World" has any semblance of life? It is given life by the invisible person. The invisible person is the foundation of life. At the same time the invisible person gives life to the "legal debt collection instrument" or "There is Nothing but a Physical World", the invisible person has the potential through it to destroy an invisible person, even self.

How is it possible that either of these ideas or concepts have any life? How is it that either of them has any force? How can either of these truly invisible concepts actually DO anything? (Note that "There is Nothing but a Physical World" is itself an invisible concept.)

Shylock used the "legal debt collection instrument" as a means or a tool to work-through to impose himself upon the Merchant of Venice. Any person, is acting as Shylock did, who uses "There is Nothing but a Physical World" as a means or a tool to work-through to impose: The key word in any case is to impose.

Chapter XI

What is the purpose of a law? If a law is not created for the purpose of being imposed, can it be labeled a law? If a description of should or ought or can is the action word, it is a principle perhaps, but not a law. Such wording may be ignored as mere advice or suggestion. A law must include an action word such as shall or will.

If a law has no warning or threat of penalty to be imposed if the law is not followed, can it be labeled a law? If there is no penalty or warning or threat of imposition, it may be ignored as mere advice or suggestion.

If no invisible person exists for a law to be imposed upon, does a law even exist? A law can only exist if the invisible person exists.

At this point, I feel abundantly confident to claim law is an invisible concept. If law was merely written and spoken symbols placed upon fabric to record those symbols and those symbols did not represent invisible concepts and require careful interpretation by an invisible person to assemble the law from the symbolic form back into the original, invisible law, then law itself would be dead. It can be exhausting attempting to fulfill the invisible law of "There is Nothing but a Physical World". To describe law as nothing but the ink on the paper is to declare law has been destroyed forever. Hence the concept (the first statement) attempted to kill or destroy the invisible person and every law ever invented.

The Invisible Person

If law can only exist if the invisible person exists, then the invisible person must be the origin of law. In fact this is true.

The entire concept of law originates from the concept of the invisible person.

Chapter XII

You can create a law for yourself and impose that law upon yourself. You can choose whether there is any threat of penalty to be imposed upon yourself and all of the rules for that penalty. You can impose the penalty in strict observance of the law or you may exercise a loose interpretation of the law with regard to the penalty.

If you later decide to eliminate the law on any basis you choose, you may do so.

This practice of creating law, imposing law, enforcing law, interpreting law, changing law and eliminating law is by definition sovereignty. You are your own sovereign person.

Law is fused to the invisible person. The invisible person is so integrated to law that seldom if ever does law even mention the invisible person.

Law is created by action (called an Act or Action). If law has action, then it must somehow have life. But law cannot have life, law cannot exist, without the invisible person. It is the invisible person or persons who give law its life. Law is a man-made creation by Man, for Man.

As the invisible person is the foundation for the existence of law, it seems very reasonable to declare any law, which attempts to destroy the invisible person, to be destructive of law itself.

Chapter XIII

The invisible person may create a law and impose that law upon self.

The invisible person may create a law and impose that law upon another invisible person. It may be a specific law imposed upon a specific invisible person. It may be a general law imposed upon a group of invisible persons or all other invisible persons.

Whether a person decides to create no such laws or create numerous such laws is again up to the sovereign person.

A person who decides to create no such laws, who decides to impose no laws upon another invisible person, is commonly described as having a "social learning disability." Such an unimposing person may appear to lash out in anger when circumstances dictate as the connection between the value/need of imposing laws upon others and achieving desired results in life is a natural connection which cannot be ignored.

A person who decides to create numerous laws and impose those laws upon others for the slightest whim/reason is considered to have many titles: Ambitious, driven, imposing, pushy, Type A, management and others.

The Invisible Person

Every culture, organization, group, family and relationship has some accepted standards for what is an acceptable amount of imposition by one invisible person upon another invisible person.

Every kingdom, government, nation, city, county and state has some accepted standards for what is an acceptable amount of imposition by one invisible person upon another invisible person.

Chapter XIV

Is it possible for another invisible person to help me and at the same time oppose me?

It is possible. It is possible whether the helpful person knowingly or unknowingly opposes me while at the same time helps me. For example, if the helpful person provided me with food, yet poisoned the food knowingly, that would be both helpful and harmful. If the food was poisoned and the helpful person was not aware of that fact, the result is no different.

If a person loans money to me, yet charges interest of 100% more upon payment, the loan may have been helpful but the interest is destructive.

If a helpful person engages in conversation with me, thereby providing some social satisfaction, and also shares with me "There is Nothing but a Physical World", have I been helped and potentially harmed? As the concept is shared over a meal in a social gathering, all may seem well and good. If the idea is unknowingly destructive of me as an invisible person was I harmed? If I lose my meaning for existence and end my life, is that the only possible damage? Is it impossible for me to be harmed as an invisible person far short of self-destruction? Or is there no relation between the meaning of life and my beliefs? And if there is no visible damage caused from the conversation, is there no damage?

The Invisible Person

In present day, the field of medicine subscribes generally to the invisible concept "There is Nothing but a Physical World". How could the physician, the medical doctor's perspective affect me, the patient? How could the doctor's perspective on the meaning of life, the science of life, the field of medicine, have any affect upon me?

If the field of medicine has imposed upon it a mandate that "There is Nothing but a Physical World", is a medical doctor allowed to stray from that mandate?

What if a law was imposed upon the field of medicine like this?: Only a man-made chemical formula can cure a person of a set of symptoms or disease. If this was imposed with the full force of government, then it must be a law. If such a law was imposed upon the field of medicine, would a medical doctor break that law by recommending a cure of any other type? Yes.

Such a law is based upon "There is Nothing but a Physical World". Why? Such a law would consider only the possibility that the field of medicine is the sole agent capable of eliminating symptoms related to health. A natural cure is therefore not allowed, by law. A medical doctor, by law, if such a law existed, could not suggest a natural cure, an approach of assisting nature in the human body. Nature has been described as "a doctor, doctoring itself."

Nature is an invisible force which is not allowed within "There is Nothing but a Physical World". If natural processes are allowed to be considered as a source of health problems or a cure of health problems, then there would be more than a physical world.

What if some health problems have natural causes? What if diabetes is naturally caused from cellular dehydration and putting oil on the feet solves the symptoms? What if hemorrhoids could be avoided by squatting fully? What if constipation is a result of cellular dehydration? What if uncooked naturally water-rich foods could re-hydrate cells and eliminate constipation and diabetes symptoms?

If natural causes exist, then natural cures exist. If "There is Nothing but a Physical World" then there are no natural causes and no natural cures.

After a story is presented which summarizes the symptoms of a health problem, and gives those summarized symptoms a name, how challenging is it for the patient to put that story aside in order to seek a summary which might more suitably fit the symptoms? If the medical doctor's story creates a "dead end" for the patient, then the patient will stop searching. In the same way, if the medical doctor found the story (research, physician's desk reference, other) and stopped searching for answers, did the medical doctor adopt a "dead end"? A "dead end" story, which gives a name to symptoms and halts the search for natural causes or natural cures, is a systemic problem. Is there any measurable cost impact to patient, to insurance, to medical doctor, to community, to nation, to Mankind?

There is a story in the field of information technology (IT) called "binary". The story about computers is that computers process "binary". Actual binary is a system of counting using two symbols, a 0 and 1. To count in binary is to begin in the same manner as any other counting system: start with 1. It is the same process for

the more commonly used decimal counting system, which uses ten symbols: 0 thru 9. All counting begins with 1. Since the very early beginnings of computers, the apparent "binary" of computers has been the story.

The impact of this story has a "dead end" aspect to it which is quite different from the medical doctor's "dead end" story, however, the same question must be raised. Is there a cost impact to the field of IT? To assist you to clearly understand why computers do not process "binary", consider a light switch. If a light switch is working correctly, there are two "states": on and off. If the light switch does not perform as expected, it is considered broken or failed (bad switch, burnt out light bulb, electricity is off). A light switch only works if it performs as expected. There is nothing random about an expected outcome.

If I lined up 2 light switches, the topic is the same. If I lined up 1,000,000 light switches, the same expectation of every switch remains the same. This is exactly how a computer works. A computer produces "switch states" or "switch state combinations".

Because of the story that computers process "binary", there has been a significant number of potential IT workers which have been unable to overcome the barrier of "binary" because all of their life they have been taught to count beginning with 1 and entering into any computer field affected by "binary", they are expected to count beginning with 0 (yep: 0 is supposed to be 1; counting is to be 0=1).

The IT field has an increasing demand for workers and this seemingly minor barrier is contributing to higher paid IT positions and fewer hiring prospects.

A medical doctor's story, a computer "binary" story: What other stories exist which create an unproductive and costly barrier?

Chapter XV

If there is no invisible person, there is no self. If this was true that "There is Nothing but a Physical World" then there would be no self, no ego. Some might exclaim, "YAY!! Ego has been destroyed!"

The very construct which, in this case destroyed the ego, is, in fact, a construct by the ego. The ego of the invisible person can create an unimaginable and uncountable number of dedications to the ego. Any construct which claims to have converted an unknowable mystery from unknowable into knowable, is likely a construct of the ego.

A magnificent building may be a tribute to a single person's ego. A poem, a story, a theory or just about any construct by an invisible person can be a tribute to a single person's ego.

"There is Nothing but a Physical World" is a construct of at least one invisible person. The construct or theory or logic or philosophy or _____ may be shared and cherished and honored, yet it is nothing more than a construct by Man, by an invisible person, and therefore a tribute to ego.

Ego did not return in this chapter. Ego never disappeared. The invisible person did remain alive and well, throughout all of time as long as the invisible person has existed, and the theory of "There is Nothing but a Physical World" did not destroy ego nor did ego

get replaced. Ego is alive and well as an aspect of self and self is an essential aspect of the invisible person.

Chapter XVI

The invisible person precedes law. Law precedes
government. Government precedes business. Where
does science fit?

Without the invisible person there would be no science.
If "There is Nothing but a Physical World", then there
would be no invisible person and therefore no science.
Yet it seems somehow science accepts "There is Nothing
but a Physical World".

Science appears to make no apologies for errors. Errors
in formulas, theories, calculations, assumptions and
predictions are advertised as merely mistakes by a
person and in no way describe a mistake by a specific
field of science. Similar to the accomplice in The
Merchant of Venice, the field of science escapes all
blame or fault, having complete freedom to fail again in
the future.

A field of science pays no penalty for a failure.

A similar idea is often found in government, businesses
and organizations. Any failure is not a failure of the
government, rather the fault/blame is _____
(person, group). Any failure is not a failure of the
business/organization, rather the fault/blame is
_____ (person, group). What is the statement?
What is the story? What is the theme?

This picture is much clearer if you simply believe "There is Nothing but a Physical World". Responsibility exists as an aspect of free-will and free-will only exists as an aspect of the invisible person. To subscribe or buy-into "There is Nothing but a Physical World" enables a disassociation from all responsibility.

As obvious as this ought to be, it must be clearly described: The invisible person exists and that invisible person has free-will and to exercise free-will is to impose responsibility upon the invisible person. The invisible person exists and that invisible person is sovereign and to exercise sovereignty is to impose a law upon the invisible person. As all man-made creations are created according to this model, every construct of Man must comply with this same model completely.

Government is a man-made construct. Government is given power of free-will by Man and therefore has responsibility imposed upon itself. Government is given power of sovereign rights by Man and therefore has law imposed upon itself. The existence of government is given to it by Man. Truly, the existence of government is not owned by government, it is strictly a loan.

Government also derives models from the invisible person such as rights, ownership and personal. Less apparent models from the invisible person are logic, reason, understanding, knowledge, wisdom, self, family and perception, yet any of these may enter the government or forum of law.

If government declared "There is Nothing but a Physical World", then government would be attempting to destroy its own existence by attempting to destroy the invisible person.

Science is also given existence by Man. Science is a man-made construct. Science is given the power of free-will by Man and therefore has responsibility imposed upon itself. Science is given power of sovereign rights by Man and therefore has law imposed upon itself. The existence of science is given to it by Man. Truly, the existence of science is not owned by science, it is strictly a loan.

Science also derives models from the invisible person such as beauty (which has many attributes itself), nature, logic, knowledge, understanding and more.

If science declared "There is Nothing but a Physical World", then science would be attempting to destroy its own existence by attempting to destroy the invisible person.

Business/Groups/Organizations is given existence by Man. Business is a man-made construct. Business is given the power of free-will by Man and therefore has responsibility imposed upon itself. Business is given power of sovereign rights by Man and therefore has law imposed upon itself. The existence of business is given to it by Man. Truly, the existence of business is not owned by business, it is strictly a loan.

Chapter XVII

What is "There is Nothing but a Physical World"? Is it a story? Is it a theory? Is it a philosophy? Is it a religion? Is it an essential belief which will place me or you in dire peril, at risk of death, if I do not believe it?

I could go from that question into whether death even matters to a person holding "There is Nothing but a Physical World" as a critical belief from which all knowledge must be brought forth. I could pursue whether any knowledge can be brought forth from that belief. Or explore the meaning of life.

I choose none of those diversions or distractions.

I choose now to explore instead a theme, a practice, a game we have all engaged many times.

The excuse:
Step 1: The process of creating a story or an account.
Step 2: The story must include a subject.
     The subject may be one or more ideas, events, actions.
Step 3: Create the story to cast the subject "in a light" of your choosing.
     A "supportive light" to characterize subject as good or justifiable or allowable or rational.
     An "unsupportive light" to characterize subject as bad/evil or unjustifiable or disallowed or irrational.
Step 4: Award the label.
     Declare the event allowed or favorable.
     Declare the idea a good idea.

Declare the idea a bad idea.

Declare the event disallowed or unfavorable.

Step 5: Await a response from the label and declaration, hoping it will be accepted.

A story, created by one person and then shared with another person in hopeful anticipation that the story will be accepted, is the theme of the all-to-common excuse. And every person throughout the existence of Man must be aware of, and experienced with, this theme. Believe what you wish, but I believe every human person ever alive has experienced the excuse theme.

Therefore, if "There is Nothing but a Physical World" follows that same theme, then any person alive can easily understand it for what it is.

Chapter XVIII

According to a story, an event or idea may be cast in a "favorable light" or an "unfavorable light". Regardless of the light or the evaluation, the story was created first.

An excuse begins with a story. A story precedes many situations, events and ideas with the expectation the story be used:

Luck: Good luck or bad luck is processed through a story of luck and actual events fit completely.

Astrology: Apparent predictions are processed through a unique story every time, and therefore actual events fit completely.

The name I have given this pre-assumption or pre-story with post-events fitting into the story completely is an Assumption Circle (or an Assumption Bubble). The key to destroy the Assumption Circle is to discover the unspoken and hidden assumptions, which are foundational and un-detachable from the Assumption Circle.

Debate about whether the luck story or the astrology story is valid or invalid by some reason of philosophy or religion is argumentative and sounds rather foolish. To mock whether an event might just as easily and completely fit as bad luck versus good luck also sounds argumentative and also sounds rather foolish.

Exploring the unspoken and hidden beliefs or assumptions, which must accompany the luck story or the astrology story is disarming and well received. What must also be believed or assumed as foundational

and un-detachable from the luck story and the astrology story?

Think about it and write it down:

_____.
      If I believe the luck story, I must also believe

      _____.
      If I believe the astrology story, I must also
      believe _____.

What are some other assumption circles, with the unspoken/hidden foundational and un-detachable assumptions, which must accompany the assumption circle?
      Fate = no free-will and _____
      Knowledge = power and _____

The Invisible Person

Chapter XIX

Until this chapter, what was presented is foundational. Whether credit must be given to another human being for any of the preceding chapters is unknown. For this chapter, I credit Anthony Robbins for providing a much needed clear and relevant description for the word "evaluate."

Mr. Robbins studied the word evaluate and discovered what it means to evaluate. It means to ask questions. A process the invisible person performs many times daily.

Using this meaning of evaluate and a few more insights, let us consider the word "fear".

Here is a scale:
Distracting –to→ Madness –to→ Trauma –to→ Coma

For some reason, a human being will enter a coma caused from too much input. Perception is an aspect of the invisible person. Perception, at a minimum, includes the five senses, proprioception, sympathy and empathy. Too much perception can range from distracting up to a coma.

Perception, upon an index finger, of temperature from cool and increasing warmer and warmer is described as sending the same signal to the brain faster and faster. As the heat increases, the signals per second to the brain increase. Literally, the person does not scream in pain because of the overheated flesh, rather the person screams due to increasing distraction to a point of

madness, and withdraws the index finger away from the heat.

For some reason, human beings are incapable of 100% focus. As far as I know there is disagreement about how many simultaneous "focuses" a human being is capable of performing or how much focus must be "assigned" to each "focus". It is safe to recognize the scale for a single "focus" and how it can affect a human being.

As perception is an invisible activity and an aspect of the invisible person, this subject makes sense to be included in this book.

There is disagreement about how fast the human brain operates. Measures attempted include words per second, brain wave patterns and more. What is relevant though is that the human being does process information very fast.

To evaluate is the process of asking questions and answering questions. It is a very fast internal process. If an evaluation process of question → answer → question → answer proceeds very fast, there seems to be no problem. For some reason, if the answer within the process results in "I don't know" or "_____" (same idea as "I don't know"), the evaluation process increases in speed, attempting to find an acceptable answer.

If the answer continues to be "I don't know" or "_____" and the evaluate process continues to increase in speed, the evaluate process enters into the scale above: distracting → madness.....

For example:

    Scenario A: A man without fighting skills is walking down a narrow alley and sees three fearsome men walking toward him. As the man approaches the three strangers, he begins to evaluate the situation. Internally he asks, "What if they do this...?" and his internal answer is, "___".

    Internally, the questions and "___" answers increase in speed and become more and more distracting, possibly to a point of madness.

    Scenario B: Same. Except the man walking toward the other three has had extensive multi-person martial arts training. As the internal evaluate process begins, "What if they do this....?" His internal answers return with confident, "Then I will do....". The evaluate process does not speed up and become distracting. What is the difference in these two scenarios? It is the evaluate process.

This is the definition of fear: To ask a question and receive the answer "_____". At first the evaluate cycle gets your attention. Next it becomes distracting. Next it becomes madness. Next it becomes disabling. After that it may be trauma, coma or complete shutdown (death). Death is the complete disconnect of the invisible person from the physical human body.

How many people ask the question about life: What will happen to me when I die? How many people get an answer other than "_____"?

Chapter XX

If the invisible person can be disconnected from the physical human body, as is apparent at complete separation or death, perhaps there are degrees of connected. If it were possible to identify measurable degrees of connected, what would such a discovery reveal?

Perhaps we have already seen a process of the invisible person becoming connected to the physical human body, and it is called conception through birth through the age of reason. Perhaps the invisible person can be more connected and less connected in changing amounts throughout the lifetime of the invisible person.

Is it possible that a more connected invisible person to the physical human body equates to better health attributes of the physical human body? Or perhaps there is no relationship between the invisible person and any degree of connected.

Regardless of such ideas, these possibilities will be completely ignored by anyone believing "There is Nothing but a Physical World."

www.ingramcontent.com/pod-product-compliance
Lightning Source LLC
Chambersburg PA
CBHW070807290526
45795CB00002B/649